For La... ...ig

MOVING WATERS

POEMS AND STORIES BY
JOHN AMBURY

*Thank you for
sharing this poetic
journey with me.
Love
John Ambury*

IOWI

Moving Waters
by
John Ambury

Published by: In Our Words Inc./www.inourwords.ca

Cover image: John Pingree

Other Images: John Pingree / RFW (sketch artist)
John Ambury / Pixabay

Editor: Cheryl Antao-Xavier

Author photo: Cheyenne Annand

Book design: Shirley Aguinaldo

Library and Archives Canada Cataloguing in Publication

Ambury, John, author
    Moving waters : poems and stories / John Ambury.

ISBN 978-1-926926-63-6 (paperback)

    I. Title.

PS8601.M38M69 2016   C811'.6   C2016-902818-6

Dedication

To the late Marion Elizabeth Talbot Ambury:
poet, philosopher, teacher, supporter, Mother.

In Appreciation

My deepest thanks for their unfailingly generous support to the many people and groups who have allowed me to read at their microphones and from their stages, and to all those who have kindly anthologized my work. My profound appreciation as well to the other special people who have helped and encouraged me at various stages along the way. These include Belle Elliott, E.S. Lilker, Lilybeth, Linda, Norma, Patrick, Thom, and Ursula. With apologies to the many I've missed!

Publishing Credits

Many of these poems (some in slightly different versions) have been published in the anthologies *Canadian Voices, Vols. 1 and 2* (BookLand Press); *Canadian Imprints, Vols. 1 and 2* (Writers & Editors Network); *The Courtneypark Connection 2013* and *The Literary Connection, Vol. 1* (In Our Words Inc.); and *Scarlet Thistles* (Beret Days Press); and in the periodicals *Verse Afire* and *News from Behind the Wheel*. The stories have not been published previously.

Introduction:
A Poem Like Unto a River

Where does a poem come from? From the writer's imagination, of course — but it has to be triggered by a thought or a feeling that demands to be expressed. One that, for some reason, needs a means of expression that's different from a plain narrative. If you're comfortable using language, and particularly if you're not adept at making pictures or music, the best means is poetry.

For me, the trigger is often an experience of love. The title poem of this collection, *Moving Waters,* uses the extended metaphor of two very different rivers coming together like a couple : beginning slowly and building to a passionate climax with the force of their combined power, before settling into a peaceful ending. This is something I couldn't express in prose, and if I tried it would fall painfully flat. That is true, I think, of most of the pieces in the book. Of course, abstract subjects such as *Lacunae* and *Quest* simply "are" poems: they'd never have a prose equivalent. The quirky or humorous pieces, especially the parodies, wouldn't work at all. (Okay, maybe the *Tomcat* pair could be converted to prose; but they wouldn't be nearly as much fun!)

The trigger can also be something that is symbolic in its own right, such as (again!) water. Other poems here use it as a metaphor, and in others it's featured in some way: something to observe or respect or meet the challenges of. But indirectly, I think most poems, however abstract or free of conventional structure, have shapes or rhythms that suggest it in some way. They might start with a small "spring" and grow to full flood. Or they might be like still ponds — or raging rapids. If they're in stanzas, they might resemble strings of paternoster lakes, connected by narrow threads; "Variations on a Theme by Robert Frost," written in that poet's linked-rhyme form, is like that.

But why limit our sources? A poem can be inspired by anything: emotional pain or delight, a painting or photograph, a political or spiritual point of view, a story or another poem; hopes or fears, history or the future, heat or cold, light or darkness, language itself. The subject or feeling may suggest a form, or you may struggle to find its most apt expression. The Muse lights on your shoulder when she feels like it, plays with your thoughts and emotions, your phrases and rhythms, according to her whim; and disembarks when it suits her (whether you have anything worth saving by then or not). You may occasionally cajole her, but you can never command her.

I describe my poems as "eclectic" (a fancy word for "as mixed-up as a hound's breakfast"), because they may be about anything, and may be any shape and almost any length. The Sections here are arbitrary — the poems came first, the attempt at organization much later — so there is, for example, some metaphor in Love and love in Metaphor. For most of the pieces, the Muse has suggested an indirect or figurative expression; but many are quite plain and straightforward. (I disagree with the poet who is quoted as having said: "Of course it's difficult. If I'd wanted it to be easy, I would have written prose." I don't want difficult, or too obscure; I want thoughtful, sometimes lighter and sometimes more profound, but always accessible.)

Wherever each poem or story starts or ends, and whether its path is direct or convoluted, each one is a journey. I hope you will enjoy accompanying me on these personal journeys.

John Ambury
Toronto, Canada
March, 2016

Contents

~ 1 ~

The Poet In Love

Blue Curves

I watch you as you sleep
the curves of your naked form
profiled in the stark blue moonlight,
reflected in the mirror, repeated in the shadows.
The epitome of nature's design
template for abstract sculptures
inspiration to millions of artists
from cave painters to Rubens to Picasso.

I watch you as you sleep
re-living in my mind our hurtful quarrel —
the phrases that turned back on each other
in recurring patterns, like cursive Möbius strips:
why did you, how could you, why didn't you?
you meant — no I didn't
but you said — yes, but — no, but …
I love you — I know, but —
escalation of spiralling emotions
with no resolution.

I watch you as you sleep
remembering how we got here:
the headlong urgency of our passion
the eager yet incremental growth of trust
the spontaneous yet cautious process
of gradually curving together into a couple.

And I watch you as you sleep
trying to understand how we got *here*
with pieces broken off and fingers burned.

I know your every curve and line
but I wonder if I ever knew *you*.

And I wonder if this will be our last night together.

(Inspired by Blue Curves, *John Pingree's photographic art
interpretation of part of a steel sculpture)*

Love, 3

Once upon a time
there was love.

Beyond the wishes for joy, oh yes
beyond the why and wherefore
beyond the cravings
such craziness
such convoluted hopeless stupid yearning
for this helpless day
together
beyond all vulgar syntax of future perfect
such foolishness all random
and sublime.

Yes, sublime.
Beyond all time
beyond all flesh, all life:
I will feel you
always.

Moving Waters

From distant springs small brooks emerge
fresh waters play, drink rain and swell, connect in streams.
Tributaries join to make a river
in quiet flow and questing flight:
a life.
Your river lives in all its streams
components, colours, temperatures
blended, but not uniform
one flood of many waters.
My river is from different springs
as complex as yours
as interwoven, yet inseparable
one stream's water from another's:
as calm where wide and smooth,
as turbulent in willful flood
but in its own path.

Our rivers meet.
They clash and turmoil, strands mix but repel
too much from upstream, too many parts
the parts are wrong.
I am not yours to absorb, you will not yield to my flow
we are not one, my heat is cold to you.

But finally
my blue reflects your green, your green takes on my hue
my warmth becomes your heat
and so we join, and move together
integrated (though not uniform)
one river of our blended waters.

After the delta will be the end, the silent end
no longer us nor any thing,
the cosmic all and nothing.

But before that, love, before!
We gently spread through meadows, slow and tranquil
embracing love as flowers …
we rage through canyons: rough-walled, harsh, confining
that cannot hold us,
shouting love as passion.
Our power together surges in torrents —
unheeding, headlong, explosive …
then calm again.

One river of all waters, we thrive
we shape the earth, we nurture, we destroy
we are wild nature, alive and free and primal
sweeping to the delta
to the end.

Love at First Sight

Love at first sight
eyes bright
hearts light
baggage heavy
heavy.

Ships that pass in the night
in the night
night.

Passion's Fire

Before the touch, the kiss; before the kiss
The words: hot verbs, bold adjectives, raw nouns
Exciting syllables that steam and hiss
Arousing turns of phrase — our mating sounds.

Between the words and kisses, clothing flies
Exposing flesh in Eden nakedness
We need our touches bare, without disguise —
The scorching grasp, the tender soft caress.

Our mouths breathe wet sensations in like air
We're animals in tune with primal beat
The jungle sounds of coupling fill our lair
Till, spent at last, we melt in panting heat.

Romance brings wondrous music to the soul
But passion's fire must rage to make love whole.

Over It

Over it?
Sure I'm over it
nothing lasts for ever, right?

Over it?
Why not, it was nothing.
Sure, it felt like something at the time —
like you'd grabbed me by the heart
and made me fall like a schoolboy
showed me how Tom Sawyer felt about Becky Thatcher
and why Romeo pined like an idiot under that balcony.
But in the grand scheme of things, it was nothing.

Over it?
Why not, I never needed you.
Even though you were the one who made me feel alive
made me want to keep you warm
made me feel I was strong and had an effect on you
made me feel wanted, needed
like I could give you something nobody else could
like I could get you past the pain
even knowing I could never be him; but not needing to be
because you wanted me for myself.

Over it?
Why not, you never loved me.
Even though you loved how I made you feel
loved that I wanted you for your heart
    and your eyes and your smile
as well as your body
loved that I waited patiently through your unsure times
loved your own responses that gave you away
under the influence of my special touches —
loved that I discovered your deepest secret desires
and met them; and loved that you could meet mine too.

Over it?
Sure I'm over it.
Even if I can't get over you.

Running Away

Run away with me
on a road to nowhere
on a subway train
on a peasant's ox-cart
on a city street
on a forest trail
guiding us

Run away with me
on wings of hope
on wings of song
on wings of eagles
on wings of guardian angels
lifting us

Run away with me
to where yesterday is long gone
to where there is no tomorrow
to where life is only today
belonging to us.

Strong

I want you strong —
believing in who you are
assured of your worth
certain of your abilities
confident of your potential
fearless.

I want you so strong in and of yourself
that you don't need me.

Then I will know
that you need me
only because you love me.

That I Can Give

Take what I have that I can give
don't ask for moon or stars
or diamond's glint
or gold.

Take what I have that I can give
don't ask for endless bliss
or a heart all yours
and true.

Take what I have that I can give
the life I've torn away
from other lives
for you.

Take what I have that I can give
the piece I keep for you
that small, bright shard
I've saved.

Take what I have that I can give
the fire that burns inside
my longing need
my self.

Take what I have, my love, that I can give –
the part that's yours
the part that makes me live.

Touches

Touches
soft as dandelion wisps
settling weightless on the skin
a fingertip stroke so slight
it might be imagined
a trace of trailing fabric barely felt
a tantalizing graze.

The scorch of fiery lightning
searing helpless flesh
stopping the heart with thunder
burning a jagged trail from scalp to toe
leaving a throbbing scar.

Touches, like warm enveloping mists
like cold waves roaring in to drown
the giddy splash of April rain
the endless drips of torture
the massage of a luxurious bath
the crashing torrent of a waterfall.

Sensations that write whole books without words
that evoke unbearable emotions
unite two searching spirits
nourish their hungry bodies
arouse their trembling senses
awaken their dormant souls.

Touches.

With Reckless Hearts

Up, up, away, a Russian shuttle jets
With Guy Laliberté in purchased berth
A clown-nosed circus stunt *sans* ropes or nets
And as per script he comes back safe to earth.

All systems go, on rockets' fearsome thrust
Columbia lifts; the earthbound watchers cheer
Exhilarated travellers rise in trust
Not knowing there's a damaged tile to fear.

The roller-coaster thrills on plunging tracks
But firmly clings to climb the higher peaks;
Icarus soars on feathered wings of wax
Then plummets, humbled by the sun he seeks.

In love we blindly leap to seize the crown,
Take flight with reckless hearts, and don't look down.

Your Rock

There is nothing new in sailing metaphors —
nothing so true or profound
that it hasn't been said before
a thousand times.

Still, I have to tell you.

I am your rock, your harbour, your lighthouse, your beacon:
you need me for a firm place to anchor, a safe haven
a light to guide you through the storm.

You are my ship:
I need you to see me, to steer to me, to need me
to make my strengths worth having.

~ 2 ~

The Metaphorical Poet

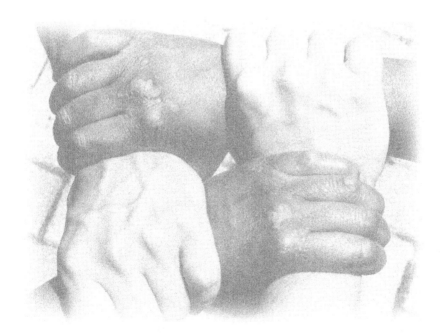

Lacunae

I exist in the world
in its three-dimensional structure
where patterns can be traced with fingertips
firing synapses make connections
trains of thought follow rails
and sentences made up of words make sense.

But I *live* in the lacunae,
the spaces between:
abstract
unreal
and patternless.

(Inspired by the multimedia artwork Zen Garden *by Derik Hawley)*

Civilization

Fritz Lang is right at home here
Tolkien plays in the towers
Orwell watches Big Brother watching
Lewis Carroll falls down the holes
Only M.C. Escher can find his way around.

But it is not imaginary:
It is Detroit and Rome and Disneyland
Dubai and Manhattan and Chichen Itza;
it is Moscow and Jerusalem and Toronto
Giza and Las Vegas and Agra.

It is past and to be, it is then and now
it is the once and future world.

It is us, manifest on the planet
our chosen dystopia
our beloved "civilization."

(Inspired by Market Church at Halle [After Feininger] *by Tsochoy Go)*

Judging Poetry

A deep pile of anonymous pages.
A great swath of creativity.
Flashes of insight; some with strange phrasings,
    awkward rhythms, unlikely images.

Read them all again. Get past the words — find the emotions.
Find the artistry, the patterns, the sculpted forms.
Hear the music; feel its triumph and beauty,
its pain and loss.

Suddenly you fall into a tumbling kaleidoscope:
all around you are colours clashing and fragments crashing;
every turn, every page, brings fresh sensations
from a thousand prisms — new spectra never seen before.

Now a richly descriptive piece, a pause for breath.
Soothing orchestral melodies and solo chords.
Still life with figures. A smile.

Then, writers' souls swirling again:
unguarded chunks and thin jagged shards
bouncing off cell walls in joy
dropping to the ground in agony
burning and freezing
discordant harmonies leaping off the pages.

Strange, awkward and unlikely are now solid materials:
abstract rock, concrete mist,
clouds and trees real but ethereal
shapes and colours only an artist can discern.
Naked bodies and exposed hearts crying and laughing
yearning to fly, struggling to conquer, to live, to survive.

Exertions finally over
you crawl the upward slope of the roller coaster.
The cogs engage safely: click-click, click-click
    slowly to the peak.
Needing to be up
so you can come down the other side,
gently back down to earth.

But down is not gentle. No railing or handhold,
a stomach-churning plunge and twist off the track
out into the unforgiving sky — and gone.

Music. Art. Poetry.

Girl in The Subway

The dark brown eyes stare out
confident but questing, frank but reserved
stairs to the stars; depth of the oceans.

Speaks Russian, they say
yes, and French too, they say.
But the language is in her eyes
those dark brown eyes
part of a smile below the untamed hair
part of an almost-smile under the straw hat —
assured or unsure, bold or withdrawn
heart-breaker or heart-broken?

She knows the book by heart — she wrote it
it is the story of everything and everybody
but I can scarce make out the meaning
deep in those dark brown eyes.

Writes poetry, they say
obscure, they say; can't be understood, they say.
They need to look into those dark brown eyes
and listen by that light.

She knows the subway.
She knows the dark tunnels, hidden levels, secret doors
she knows the ancient beast that lurks there.
No flute to make her music —
the magic is in her mystical eyes
and in the hand-spun phrases
she weaves on her fantastical loom.

Can't be understood, they say.
They need to look into those dark brown eyes
and listen by that light.

(For Tali de York, in response to her poem Girl with a Flute)

Poet

They read your poems.

They have felt that music
feared that ocean storm
thrilled to that very passion
wept at that lover's leaving —
they marvel that you've discovered their emotions
and evoked them with just words.

They hear your voice on the page.
Smiles spread. They like you.

They read again.

These are not descriptions
of the Grand Canyon, or the trumpet, or your father.
Shapes and colours are not defined.
You soar above and delve beneath the surface senses
your lines bring to their hunger
not how things look or sound
but how they *are* to you
in your most secret confessions:
your joy and pain and fear
longing, wonder, uncertainty
love and lust
despair and hope —
your heart and your guts
exposed, laid bare.

They hear you whisper
Be here with me; see this in me; can you feel it too?

They touch your soul on the page.
Tears burn. They love you.

(for Saskia van Tetering, on her collection After Philosophy*)*

Quest

Come with me on my quest —
we have nothing to lose
but life and its shackles.

Come, cross the wintry North Atlantic
in a birch canoe, tight-sewn by native hands
old now and cracked, but surely sound enough
to crest the white-capped waves and skim the troughs
to save the world.
    Wild gales and tempests drown our petty craft
    Titanic floats, green mermaids flash their tails
    we navigate canals of blood-red Mars
    unhindered.

Come, brave Sahara's sun-scorched sands
on a dromedary, worth gold when she was young
old now and lame, but surely strong enough
to plod the dunes and trek the endless wastes
to save the world.
    A sandstorm buries us in drifted mounds
    El Lawrence rides, flame-steeded nomads soar
    we dance on cratered lush moonscapes
    unweighted.

Come, conquer snow-peaked Everest
in Hillary's boots, the finest ever made
old now, worn down, but surely firm enough
to scale the rocks and leap each broad crevasse
to save the world.
    A roaring avalanche sweeps us away
    lost climbers fly, a choir of Sherpas sings
    we ski on Neptune's shining glaciers
    unfettered.

We have nothing to lose
but life and its shackles —
come with me on my quest.

Teepee Woman

From the mists that thread the pines
from the smoke of sweetgrass smudges
from the earliest passed-down legends
come the ancient symbols.

They appear and combine
separate and re-blend
shape-shifting into forms that hold the world,
patterns that explain the skies;
solid as oak
fluid as water
ethereal as a dream.

You know the mysteries, Teepee Woman
you see the meanings
you hear the answers.

With my brittle, literal, civilized intelligence
I can barely imagine the questions.

Tell me what is real
Teepee Woman.

(Inspired by the acrylic abstract Teepee Woman and Blue Pyramid
by Azhar Shemdin)

The Last Day

No sound.
Sitting on the floor
hunched over
cat on his lap
throat slit
still warm
hot blood flowing everywhere pooling
sharp knife in his limp hand
inconsolable tears
but no sound
no sound.

The last day.

The Poets: B. P.

What pressures you to sing?
       Is it aching for life lost
       for time not spent with your son
       for not returning lovers' clinging?
or is it needing to shout from the slums of Cambodia
what you feel, but don't know,
what happens when lightning shudders your bones
when emotions ignite your synapses
       The hauntings that tear you apart
and hold you together
as you lose your breath yet speak?

(For Brandon Pitts, on his collection Pressure to Sing.
Form devised by him for his seven-stanza tribute poem The Poets)

Trial By Fire

Bring yourself here, to this sacred place
where reality is shaped and truth is born
where your life will be defined
by facts and fears, fiction and fate, ignorance and irony.

Inhale this meditative atmosphere
where the icons are free, soaring birds
where the colour of existence is the calm azure of the sky
where you can rest and float and breathe.
Bathe in the coolness of the blue ether
feel it soothe your skin.

Or,
walk down the corridor and into the flames —
we seek justice in fire: it refines and cleanses.
Surrender your naked flesh
to the scorching and scalding and broiling.
Scream in pain like Joan, when there's no turning back
clutching a crude cross in vain desperation
gloating eyes rejoicing as your blood sizzles —
like modern Hebrew children, when no angel came
like the people of Nagasaki and Dresden and Coventry.
Planes into towers, torched villages and markets
incendiary rockets and napalm and necklacing
arsoned nightclubs, charred bodies stacked against chained
    doors
infidel-roastings in Castile and Salem and Papua New
    Guinea.
Feel the hottest horrors of Hell
like every soul who dies in fiery agony.

But do not die.
Stay in the heat for ever
disappeared, nameless and alone
praying for the release of death
that will not come.

Endure the endless torture
the branding, the rape with hot irons
bamboo alight under fingernails
hands and feet buried in glowing embers
who would not say *anything* to make it stop?
But it will not: the cause justifies the means —
state-sanctioned anti-terrorism measures
or anti-state rebels and freedom fighters;
for faith, or truth, or power, or even sport —
the burning is the same. And it does not stop.

Or,
inhale this meditative atmosphere
where you can rest and float and breathe.
Bathe in the coolness of the blue ether
feel it soothe your skin.

To A Lump Of Coal

O, tiny black and dirty lump of coal!
In solitude upon the cellar floor
You sit, aloof from me, quite undisturbed
By hearing the great, hungry furnace roar.
    You know what fate would soon be yours if I
    Should open wide that fire-restraining door
    And pick you up and hurl you, as I might
    Into the leaping fire's bright, red-hot core;
Yet my soliloquy you quite ignore,
As though my talk to you were such a bore.

And though you are, you dirty little thing,
A measly piece of coal, and nothing more,
You might teach to this world of foolish men
Of your most comprehensive, simple lore.
    For we should learn, when faced with fate unkind,
    To think not of our sad misfortune sore,
    But only do our best, our very best,
    In any difficult position, for
Just think to what great heights this world might soar
If we, as you, would cruel fate ignore!

(High school Senior First Prize, 1954. This shows what can be achieved by a teacher-pleasing inspirational message with consistent metre and a clever rhyme scheme!)

Trinity: The Great Oak

The branches are heavy with leaves
lush with growth and energy
spreading earth-wide
displaying the essence of life.
The vast canopy dominates the landscape
dwarfing lesser species:
an overwhelming presence,
a grand cathedral dome.

Beneath the ground, unseen,
as wide and far as the branches' reach
the vast network of roots
delves into the earth
extracting from the soil below
essential nutrients and moisture
feeding the whole being
giving foundation and counter-balance
to the powerful mass above
enabling the acorns, the next generation.

Between the two,
connecting the proud display to its hidden source,
the trunk rises from the land
a solid pillar thrusting skyward
firmly owning its place
a symbol of effortless strength
and permanence:
the monarch serene in his might,
his immense and weighty crown
a mere trifle to bear.

Can three such different parts be only one:
one entity, indivisible?

The great oak, in its unified splendour,
proclaims the answer.

Variations on a Theme by Robert Frost

Whose words these are I surely know
His resting place is distant though —
He will not see me delving here
Within his mind's old piles of snow.

The darkest evenings of the year
Bring conscience bleak and futile tear
There is no solace in the night
Nor peace, nor warmth, nor comfort, near.

Who knows which road wends dark or bright?
Just, one is left and one is right.
Too late we find which way turns sour
And which stays sweet with love's delight.

The last remaining golden flower
I offer you this final hour
Its petals fading into dust
The sad recall of summer's bower.

When memory turns to love and lust
I stumble on old words of trust
I feel the frost of vows bought cheap
Blown in on every wintry gust.

Through every crack the chill drafts creep
Regrets are drifted cold and deep.
What promises might I yet keep
With so few miles before I sleep?

~ *3* ~

The Quirky Poet

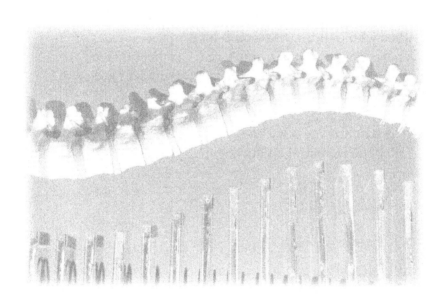

Bees

I think that I shall never see
A poem wondrous as a bee
A bee who soars with grace and flair
And does the honey-dance in the air

To show his mates he's found the way
To the gardens that are best today
For gathering nectar in the bowers
(And pollinating all the flowers).

A bee who, some say, cannot fly
Yet beelines surely through the sky
To light upon each blossom's rim
And sip the treasure found within.

A bee who builds a wax-comb hive
Where the queen holds court, and wee bees thrive;
Where he stores those hard-earned pounds of honey
That people steal and exchange for money.

Do not annoy the busy bee —
If riled, he may sting poets like me!

(With apologies to Joyce Kilmer)

Buddy, Can You Paradigm?

(Sung to the tune of Buddy, Can You Spare a Dime?*)*

Now there's just one pronoun we all know:
"You," we say "you" all the time
Plural or singular, subject or no
Buddy, can you paradigm?

Chorus 1:
    Don't you remember Elizabeth One?
    "Your" was all clear in her time!
    "Thy" was in vogue then; and I've just begun
    Buddy, can you paradigm?

Once there were "thou" and "thee," which Shakespeare used
Singulars, good for a rhyme
Now it's just "you" (maybe "you guys" or "youse")
Buddy, can you paradigm?

Pronouns once were elegant — people said
Possessive: "Thy coat is thine"
Now they say "Your coat is y'all's coat" instead
Buddy, can you paradigm?

Chorus 2:
    Don't you remember the King James tome,
    Verse and chapter divine?
    "Ye" was in vogue then; and my song is done
    Buddy, can you paradigm?

(On the paradigm [set of forms] of the English second person pronoun. The use of "paradigm" as a verb is a neologism.)

Canada Post Blues

'Twas the week before Christmas and all through the mail
Not a Postie was walking, not even a snail
You think you'll be sending those cards from your house?
You better start e-mailing, clicking that mouse!

Letterboxes? — old-fashioned, at least at your door
Take a jaunt to that mass mailbox down by the store
You'll be getting your exercise: "ParticipAction"
And meeting your neighbours, catching up on the action.

So the rates are increasing in wild increments?
They'll make even more money to pay Presidents!
Yes, they'll get rid of carriers, that's a sure fact,
But all the *executives*' jobs are intact.

Get ready to drive to a Drug Mart location
They've closed down retail at the local Post station
You can still pick up packages there, don't be nervous:
But only till 12 noon — now, *there's* some great service!

Another thing's changing: they want to charge more
For mailing to Postal Codes not near your door
We'll send fewer letters, revenues will decline
So we'll pay gold for parcels, which we can't ship on-line.

These changes were all recommended to follow
By outside consultants: not too hard to swallow …
Never mind that our Postal Corp.'s own CEO
 - is on the Board of the "independent" consulting firm
  - that made these recommendations TO him —
   - so he could recommend to himself
    - what he'd already decided to do!
That made his choice easy — at least, now we know!

It's plain that it's conflict of interest, writ large;
Does Ottawa care? — nah, just pay what they charge!
Well, Chopra, we can't wait to hear your next news —
We can add a new verse to the *Canada Post Blues!*

"Für Elise"

His presence fills the office halls
from nine to five
Beethoven calls;

He haunts the place throughout the day
his music will
not go away.

That tinny tune from
our new Xerox,
yes, we all think
it's a blight ......

"Come, do your job!" is what it says,
"Fill up my trays,
And do it right!"

(Inspired by Xerox, *melody by Beethoven)*

It's Handy

That extremity with its opposable thumb
and its prehensile digits
ranks us right up there
with chimps and baboons and sloths;
gives us a whole range of activities
that other species are denied.

Just off-hand:
stage hands, dishpan hands
hand jive, high five
chopping trees, raising bees
picking nits, knitting mitts
surgery, technology
hand-span, grab what you can
hand job, turning a knob
hand tools, polishing jewels
painting and sculpture, all kinds of culture
texting and tweeting, waving a greeting
shaking a hand, shoveling sand
grasping a sword, clambering aboard
height of a horse, piano of course
knuckle ball — and that's not all.

In addition, an endless trove of symbolism:
hand up or handout
hands-on or hands-off
hands down or Hands up!
hand-me-downs or hand of cards
hands on the wheel or all hands on deck
your hand in marriage, a hand of applause
pinching a penny, weaving a web
ring finger, middle finger
thumbs up, thumbs down
dextrous or sinister
(or, on the other hand — ambidextrous!)

Very handy, that hand!

Tomcat, One

I wake, stretch, yawn
vaguely remember Missy from last night
think about picking up my sniff-mail from the trees
but it can wait
let's see who has breakfast out for me!
Wonder if these humans know who's eating it?
who cares? — I scarf it down.

Okay, the mailbox
but wait, a little luxurious grooming first
ahh, lovely — purrrrrr!
Must be time for my morning nap.

Okay, the mailbox.
Seems Fluffy had another litter
Fluffy? — oh yeah, that smoky-grey Persian … I think
always was a bit loose
fun in her way, but careless
guess she's back in circulation now!
Tilly — is she the orange tabby?
wild thing, no wonder she's expecting.
No morals around here any more!

Seems Lionel lost part of his other ear
a fighter, that one, not a lover!
who cares about territory?
there's plenty of pussies to go around
of course, he doesn't have my suave tuxedo looks
or my irresistible singing:
gets them every time.

No way those are my kids, Booboo
are they black and white? no, I didn't think so
anyway, you never even looked back
over your shoulder that night
I wasn't born yesterday.

Hmm, trouble —
Willie's mad, thinks I banged his lady.
Who knows, it's dark at night!
guess I have to leave a message for Lionel,
straighten Willie out for me.

Better have my afternoon nap
another busy night ahead!

Tomcat, Two

(Same cat, quite a few years later)

I wake, yawn, stretch
joints are getting creaky!
vaguely remember singing on the fence last night
nobody listening.

Think about picking up my sniff-mail from the trees
but it can wait
a scrounged breakfast and a good BM are more urgent.

Okay, mailbox. But first, my first morning nap.

Right, mailbox.
I try to keep up, but I hardly know these cats
maybe knew their great-grandfathers
(or mothers, more likely)
but who can keep track?
Lionel bought it — lasted a long time for a scrapper.
Tilly's gone domestic — what a waste!
I had posted: "Anybody for a singing contest?"
No replies.

You try to teach what you've learned
these kids don't know from squat
but will they listen?
they just want pussies galore.
There's more to life than that —
singing! poetry! philosophy! bird-watching!
Okay, the occasional piece gives you a smile
(if you can get it up),
and maybe a few more offspring.
When you have perfect genes it's only fair to pass them on!
Soon be past it, though ....

What a long day. Better have my afternoon nap.

Tonight? I don't think I'm in voice, Sammy.
Ask me again tomorrow, okay?

Not too early.

Ode To A Fear-Mongering Tree-Hugger

Suzuki said we'd clear-cut all the hills
We'd have no oxygen to feed our sprawl
But I saw seedlings planted by the mills:
Perhaps Suzuki didn't know it all!
  Yet water, trees and air are getting tight —
  Perhaps Suzuki really had it right?

Suzuki said the tar sands were a mess
And cars' exhaust the planet's death would bring
But God gave us that oil, our lives to bless:
Perhaps that wise guy didn't know a thing!
  Yet now our fragile world begins to croak —
  Perhaps Suzuki knew whereof he spoke?

Suzuki said we'd foul the seas with crap
We'd have no water clean enough to drink
But melting glaciers soon filled my tap:
Perhaps the "expert" needs another think!
  Yet now the earth's condition does appall —
  Perhaps I should have listened, after all!

4

The Random Poet

Brothers By Chance

Prisoners of the Barriefield bus
a pacifist's son and an army brat
outsiders thrown together
brothers by chance.

Bluejeans and bomber jackets
defying the V-neck pullover code
quiet iconoclasts, rebels without a target
always asking why, not wanting an answer.

KCVI: *Maxima Debetur Pueris Reverentia*
Murray rules, Kelly scowls
Belle Elliot slings iambic pentameter
Sexy Smith swings her French legs
Maybee for music, drama with Grass
sonnet for the Coronation, triple-tongued clarinet
self-taught guitar, ode *To a Lump of Coal*
Ed Sullivan or Sid Caesar
flying or marching
divergent inspirations, aspirations.
And was she really so painfully, breathtakingly beautiful,
    that girl we both yearned to dance with?
        And what was her name, anyway?

My blue Hillman nearly killed me
decades later your Yamaha bike tried it on you
(though you were sober).
Your black Hillman on the gravel driveway
your father's wire-wheeled TR-3
tonneau cover and winter hardtop
your mother's fore-and-aft Studebaker
(what was behind our Army housing, a '48 Pontiac?)
later you retro-fitted reclining seats for a shaggin' wagon
I could hardly change a tire
my carved model was a Caddy, yours a concept
projects we never finished.

Martello tower submarine races
Cartwright Point, walks with Dalmatian Duchess
hourly labour on the stone wall
poison ivy and calamine lotion
sweet on your cute kid sister
knocked you out with Gary's gloves
double dates for formals and shows
pennies thrown at us in the movie
downside of being a teacher's kid.

Four theatres there were back then
CKWS-TV in "compatible black and white"
Amey's and Modern are still cruising
Regiopolis and Notre Dame merged
Whig-Standard gone corporate
city sprawled all over the Township.

The scientific mind went to the bank
the literary one to radio, then the lab
lifetime careers that weren't to be
another drummer always called
and authority rankled.
Independent and different
settled for and settled down:
classic overly-clever underachievers.

The agnostic moved north
learned Portuguese and got religion
the penitent moved west
lost his faith and scorned the Crown;
and the moving finger, having writ, moved on.

Have we lived up to our potential?
Maybe, maybe not.
But we have lived.

(For Denny: Kingston, Ontario, 1950s)

Ice Storm

It came overnight as freezing rain —
fell wet, then froze on everything
covered every fencepost and bough and snowdrift
with a thick oppressive coating of solid ice.
Broke off big tree-limbs with its weight
took down power lines.

The next morning there was no sun
to make those sparkling-diamond ice photos
    you see sometimes —
just shades of grey: iron and pewter and tarnished silver.

Down by the back fence lay a small dark shape
on the hard-crusted snow.
Turned out to be a black squirrel, frozen.
Never made it to his safe cozy home
high up in a wind-cracking maple:
just an unheated nest of dry leaves and twigs
but warm with his family's body heat.

Bitter cruel cold. The heat was off for several days,
most of the week in some places.
Joanne down the street survived
by wearing her mink coat to bed
some of us stayed with family or friends
or huddled in school gyms.
A few died — a few people
with no resources, no options.
Not many, but it made the news.
I didn't know them.

I didn't know the squirrel either
but somehow he was my neighbour, my clan.
I shuddered,
feeling the ice crystals slowly solidifying his blood
the desperate freezing of his flesh after he fell
and mostly, his hopelessness.

His death was the one that touched me most.

Layers, Subconscious

(Inspired by the mosaic Dark Seascape *by Jean Loney)*

Layers of meaning
meanings in a dream
dreams of a dark seascape.

Yes: indigo sky
over turquoise waves
over ultramarine swells
over octarine secrets
over amber sand;
and below, far below
prehistoric basalt formations
over dead black igneous bedrock,
solid and immutable.

But no: this is a dream —
the layers only seem to make sense.
Prismatic, flowing and swirling,
they are dense with finely-detailed imagery:
abstract, emotional, and profoundly … meaningless.

In the nightmare
the firm foundation is in the amorphous sky and water —
the drowning is in the treacherous shifting rock
the sea-scuffed pebbles
the water-polished marbles
the life-abandoned shells
the sharp-edged cutting gravel.

The drowning is in the inhaling
of dirt and stones and grit
the breathing-in of dry elements with no oxygen,
no sustenance, no life force.
None.

The drowning is in the desperate gasping for air
that is not here
that never will be here
in this mysterious dark seascape.

Disney Lied

No kiss awakes the dead.
There is no talking cricket
no flying elephant
no metamorphing pumpkin
no Beast made princely.
There is no wicked witch thwarted
no dragon slain.

Wish upon a star? see where that gets you
Santa Claus? ask a ghetto orphan
Tinkerbell? a glint of illusion
Easter Bunny? a chocolate trickster
Tooth Fairy? a night prowler.
All phoney.

The magic wand is a powerless stick
magic ring a bit of metal
magic cape a scrap of fabric
magic elixir a fool's quaff
magic spell a useless phrase.
All phoney.

El Dorado is a leaden slag-heap
Fountain of Youth a stinking sewer
Bluebird of Happiness a carrion crow.

There is no Arizona
no gold at the end of the rainbow
no Shangri-La
no Paradise.

We live in vain, we die in despair.

And yet we hope —
always, always we hope.

My Path

You say I am old.
Yes, my son, I *am* old.

You say my path is behind me:
lived, trodden, finished.

Yes, my past path *is* behind me
as yours is behind you;
but my future path lies before me
as yours lies before you.

Short or long, it is mine to walk
mine to explore at my own pace
mine to see to its next bend
to its next fork
to its final gate.

Yes, my son, I am old;
but I am not dead —
I live, as you live.

Do not bury me
while my path still lies before me.

(Inspired by the photo art The Journey *by John Pingree)*

Raven

A wise elder once told me
on the evidence of his half-blind eyes
and his arthritic fingers on my cheek
that my totem animal is Raven.

"Same as a crow, isn't it, only bigger?"

Quoth Milton Acorn:
"You can imitate the call of the crow
but not the call of the raven." [1]

You can imitate the soul of Crow
but not the soul of Raven —
redeemer of the darkened Sun
rescuer of the stolen Moon
guiding light to lost lovers
jester to the very Heavens.

In creation, when totems had power.

Nevermore.

[1] In Love and Anger: Milton Acorn - Poet. *National Film Board, documentary by Kent Martin, 1984.*

Root Beer Days

Countless years ago
summer was as it should be:
too hot, too free, too painless
too innocent.

You remember — that short time between wars
between child and adult
when sarsaparilla was ancient history
before Snapple was invented —
those achingly sweet root beer days.

From September to June, boys became men
in maths and science and shop classes,
in Cadets and competitive sports;
but in the summer, by absorbing their fathers' lore.

Watching horses through knotholes
warned against gambling on them;
hunting, warned against playing with guns;
fishing, warned against barbed hooks and undertows;
warned against hard drink
and careless coupling and cowardice.

But never warned
against watching girls walk with hips swaying
or dance with circle skirts flying
or sunbathe with lanky limbs extended
and budding chests striving to be noticed.

Or sports like girls' softball:
yes, a few moments of almost sexual intensity —
but in between, all the sweet time in the world
for leisurely watching. Slowly becoming men

in those far-off root beer days.

Scene with Birches

Tom Thomson was here
moving alone through these woods
rucksack on his back
images shifting in his mind
seeing this the way he or Jackson or Varley did
not the way you and I do.

Tom Thomson was here
stepping back for perspective
seeking the one vantage point
from which he could see the composition
take shape and come together.
Ansel Adams said
it's all about knowing where to stand
where to place the tripod, or the easel.

Tom Thomson was here
sitting quietly on his canvas stool
sorting tubes and brushes and knives.
He closed his eyes for darkness,
then opened them, to see the picture
fresh-lit in front of him
needing only his inner sight and his guided hand
to make it appear on the board, interpreted.

Tom Thomson was here
making the birches live:
with sure unhurried strokes
portraying the scene
as no one had ever seen it before.

Tom Thomson was here.
A few days later
his body was found in Canoe Lake.

(Inspired by a photograph of birch trees by Derik Hawley)

Sidewalk Artist

The sidewalk artist does not fear the rains.

He only awaits them, in an abstract way —
as he awaits the far-distant call of his own mortality
as he awaits the eventual shrivelling of the dandelion
in the crack in the concrete
barely noticing, in passing, the pure parachutes of new life
it sends drifting to the next street,
    the next meagre crevice.

He too drifts to the next street,
    the next raw canvas.

(For David Kane, who describes himself as "A scholar of the abstract ... an artist, chalking the sidewalks as I go, awaiting the rains to begin again.")

Smog Alert, Toronto

It's the nature of things
welcome to the big city
two-and-a-half million people, what do you expect?
We all have to get where we're going
and we need our deliveries;
life must go on, right?
    Breathe.

I could do my part I guess
I could take the subway
streetcar, GO train, hybrid bus
no problem making electricity —
just natural gas and nuclear
so it's all clean and green, right?
But I'm in a hurry today, can't be helped
damn Gardiner construction
Don Valley congestion
belching diesels blocking the lanes
cyclists with face masks.
    Breathe.

Maybe I will red-rocket next time —
filthy swaying trains
closed-circuit eyes
graffiti on the backs of buildings
hypnotic clickety-clack
horrible screeching of wheels
ghastly lighting
pushy, sweaty crowds
ghostly dead stares, grimly-set scowls
my environmentally-friendly enemies.
    Breathe.

"Yonge subway line closed
Bloor Street to Dundas station,
shuttle buses running."
No problem
just another summer suicide
can't be helped
a hiccup in the nature of things.
    Breathe.

"Hot, humid, hazy,
air quality index in the high-risk range."
But it's nothing serious
happens all the time
it's just the weather
low pressure most likely
or high pressure, who knows
anyway, it can't be helped
it's the nature of things: suck it up.

Welcome to the big city.
    Breathe.

(Inspired by an experimental brush-pen sketch by Derik Hawley)

The Guru

After a difficult and dangerous climb
an ordeal of many hours
I finally achieve the peak.

The bearded guru sits cross-legged
at the mouth of his bare stone cave
clad in homespun rags
unwashed, unkempt, unworldly.

I stare at the dirty scrap of parchment he gives me.
"That's it? That's all there is?"

He shrugs.
"You expected — what?"

"I don't know. Something … more profound!"

"Ah." He nods. "Something deep and philosophical.
All the wisdom of the ages. The meaning of life."

"Yes! Well, at least something I didn't already know!"

"Ah. But what you already know is all there is to know.
Can you not understand that?"

"No! You were supposed to … tell me something new!"

"Ah, new." He sighs. "Hear my words, my pupil:
There *is* nothing new.
It is as it always has been.
It is as it always will be.
All the wisdom of all the ages is on that paper."

I stare at the dirty scrap of parchment.
I read it again, carefully:
As you find it, so it is. Make of it what you will.

"You mean, like … it is what it is, get over it?"

"I mean: 'As you find it, so it is. Make of it what you will.'
Go safe, my pupil. Namaste."

"Goodbye, Master."
There is nothing more to say.
I turn, and begin the long, lonely journey
back down the mountain.

Spring on the Pond

Animation suspended
no life in snow.

Just days from now this pond will teem
with newborn beings
to stock the world
with every species
    two by two in billions
        the genesis of all existence.

But now the pond lies still.

No life in snow
animation suspended.

(Inspired by the oriental brush painting Early Spring [Spring on the Pond]
by Baoxing Zhang)

5

The Seventeen-Syllable Poet

(Haiku, Senryu)

YIN

YANG

Finding the Art

Note:

I know nothing authoritative about "haiku" — I can only go by what I've read, and some of that is contradictory. Interpreting Japanese traditions involves understanding culture and philosophy more than it does translating words.

There are several ways of attempting the form in English. The most common formula, which I follow, is using 17 syllables in three lines of five, seven and five syllables. Haiku have minimum punctuation, abbreviated syntax, and no rhyme or metre. Ideally the third line (or the second part) presents an abrupt change — a surprise or twist in content or viewpoint from the first part. I respect that ideal but don't always observe it.

I disregard the tradition of making the meaning so profound that it is obscure. Many of my haiku do not deal with nature or the seasons, which I am told makes them "senryu" rather than "haiku." A tradition I do usually follow in public readings is to read each piece twice — this allows the listener to hear the second part with a full appreciation of its context.

The form
Expose deepest soul
explore widest universe
only three short lines

Titles
Haiku I am told
must not be given titles —
your indulgence, please

Wabi Sabi

Note: Wabi sabi is, loosely, the oriental philosophy that an object with imperfections (such as those resulting from hand-crafting or age and use) has character, which makes it more beautiful than if it were "assembly-line" flawless.

Felicity
> Awkward birth defect
> always walks with sideways limp
> like all perfect cats

Car
> First dent, she panics
> he shrugs; a million grey cars
> now ours is unique

Cup
> One cup of twenty
> a small chip from years of use
> this one I like best

Contrail
> Ideal sunset glow
> marred by curving aircraft streak:
> art superimposed

Darkroom
> Silver halide print
> near-invisible tong mark
> craftsman's hand revealed

Doorway
> Hours to paint door frame
> deepest beauty is scratched in:
> ladders of kids' heights

Primitives
        Painter's perception
        crude figures, no perspective
        art is not drafting

Quilt
        New that very week
        faint love stain stays years later
        still makes them both smile

Rug
        Here the dog turned round
        lying down his fourteen years
        worn place brings sadness

Nature and Ecology

Note: These were written for Canada Blooms (Water and Re-wilding Project), *2014.*

Aboriginals
>People once lived here
>in harmony with nature —
>they were savages!

Amends
>Mending our damage
>who will take that first small step?
>it begins with me

Big city
>Concrete, glass and steel
>bear witness to our power
>parks and trees show love

Chaos theory
>So little to start
>the ladder of destruction:
>we are butterflies

Ecosystem
>Billions of species
>share a fragile balanced globe
>people are but one

Endless
>Water is endless
>it is there, right from the tap
>until it is not

Pollution
> Clear streams and rivers
> sacred sources of all life
> we use as sewers

Re-wilding
> Water flows, plants grow
> bees and ducks and deer return
> now a better place

Love and desire

Absence
> "I love you, miss you"
> cold words freeze-dry on my screen
> hot tears brim my eyes

Balm
> Soul and being ache
> living is defined by pain …
> love works its magic

Beach
> No perfect white sand
> tourists scorn the gravel shore
> we have privacy

Book
> Read once, almost new
> but dog-eared at her favourite
> erotic passage

Desire
> I wish to explore
> your profound and complex mind
> and screw your brains out

Perfection
> If you were perfect
> I could not match that standard
> you are right for me

Zatsuyou (miscellaneous)

Communication
>So she goes, *Duh, right?*
>I'm like, *Tell me about it*
>She's like, *Just sayin'*

Jesus Christ Superstar
>Mortals strive for fame
>superstars bask in glory
>how strange — Jesus wept

Poetry
>We do not make art
>sky-thrown hearts fly back in words
>poetry happens

Tsunami
>Apocalypse now
>forty days and nights of floods
>how shall we still breathe?

~ 6 ~

The Prose Poet

Brothers in Arms

L ate for lunch on the Interstate South. Not good planning — I'm hungry and it's a long way to the next rest stop.

But there are signs on giant poles — Next Exit, Exit NOW — Food, Gas, Motel, Adult DVDs. Magic Mountain, Gas, Food, Class A Mechanic on Duty. More food, more fuel. I think of the old quip, "Eat here and get gas."

Truck Stop: Diesel, Hearty Meals, Beds. They used to say, if you want a good meal, eat where the truckers eat — they know best.

I navigate the exit ramp, bounce along the tire-rutted entrance, and snake around the gigantic tractor-trailers and straights. Most are proud and shiny, some are dusty from travel, a few are rough and work-worn. Finally, I find the few four-wheeler spots. Guys are smoking outside — sharing tall tales, no doubt: traffic woes or vehicle woes or woman woes. I can't guess which guy is hauling the livestock, or the ready-mix or lumber, or the secret cargoes hidden inside trailers and under lumpy tarps.

I try to walk in like I belong. But I might as well be from another planet. Big overweight guys, lean sinewy guys, taut weight-lifter types; not much in between. Long hair, curly hair, uneven brush cuts, short pigtails. Lots of caps, some cowboy hats. Dozens of tattoos. Testosterone city.

The booths are *Reserved for Professional Drivers on Duty.* They offer *Free Wi-Fi* and *Free Phone Charging.* You can *Read all the papers you want but please leave them for the next customer.* Heart-broken country music is blaring from the speakers. Soups are slopped over the oilcloth, self-serve apple and coconut-cream pies are destroyed, the salad bar has been picked at. Dirty plates and coffee cups are strewn around waiting to be picked up. I find a stool at the counter, open a menu.

Coffee, honey?
Yes please.
Know what you want?
Give me a minute, okay?
Sure thing, honey.

Burgers, fried chicken, steak, pork chops. Lots of things with gravy, everything with fries or mashed except the spaghetti. Mixed veg or chef salad included, soup or salad bar extra, homemade pies extra. Bottomless coffee. She fills my mug with steaming black brew in a practiced two-second pour, not spilling a drop.

Decided, honey?
I'll have the Salisbury steak, please.
Have the hot hamburg, save you a couple bucks, you can have pie.
Okay, sure.
Fries, chef salad, right?
Uh, yes, right.
Soup, split pea or French onion?
No thanks.
Gotcha, honey. Comin' right up.

Her badge says *Esther.* I guess I was expecting *Dolly-Mae* or something. Stereotypes. I try not to watch the muted news channel — urgently flashing images, meaningless without context.

He threw in some onion rings, no charge.
Tell him thanks for me.
Sure thing, honey.

The hot hamburger is a big greasy patty between two thick slices of plain white bread. Lots of salty gravy, quickly congealing. The hot coffee might help wash it down. A huge pile of limp fries, also greasy. Eat where the truckers eat — right.

I eat the patty, the no-charge onion rings of course, some of the bread and gravy. I pick at the fries (ketchup added), while I scan the local paper. High school baseball and basketball teams are mostly winning, footballers are in a slump. Weddings and engagements, funerals, family reunions, lost dogs. Coffee keeps coming: thanks, Esther. Too full for pie. She gets a nice tip.

One of the roughest-looking truckers pays his bill just before me. Twice my size and more, belly hanging over his belt. Viet Nam Vet cap on his greasy hair, U.S. Marine Corps tattoo on his bulging bicep. Wouldn't want to meet him in a dark alley.

After paying I browse my way through the magazines and trucker gear to get to the front. A sudden storm has blown in. Rain is pelting down in buckets from the black sky. I turn my collar up and push through the door. There, under the overhang, stands the out-of-shape Marine veteran: wet-shirted, incongruous-looking Arnold Palmer Classic golf umbrella gripped in his ham-sized fist.

Hey, you! Here!

Holding the umbrella over me protectively, he splashes us through the puddles to my car, the only family sedan in sight.

Thanks a lot! I shout over the pounding rain, clambering in. But he and Arnold Palmer have disappeared into the downpour. I wonder what could have inspired his good deed.

I turn on the ignition, then the headlights and wipers. Terrible visibility. I back up extra carefully, watching all the mirrors and looking over my shoulder.

That's when I notice my old Army Reserve cap on the back window ledge.

Chaudhury's Concept

We're sitting in a small informal group, trying to follow him.

I'm present in body, but only partly in mind. I have a deadline to meet and my script, already optioned by the network, is refusing to come together. It's a jumble. I know the ideas are sound, down to the last character traits and plot twists ; but the scenes won't gel or mesh. I wish I could just throw everything against the wall, and have the manuscript put *itself* together and magically slide into my laptop.

Crazy. I give up and tune in to the discussion.

He's enthusiastic about his idea *(it may not even be original, but it intrigues me!);* but frustrated with the difficulty of putting it into words. He tries again.

Think of something like … a tall column — his expressive hands demonstrate — *maybe this high. Divided into three parts.* His slim brown fingers slice across once, twice.

Each part expands sideways — palms outward, hands pushed towards the walls to illustrate it — *maybe also front to back, in the other dimension, that would give layers. Each expanded part is made up of many, many scenes. Beginnings are at the top; endings at the bottom. The middle is filled with … with development scenes: moving bits that fit in some ways, not in other ways. Randomized, free-floating. Able to shift around and sort themselves into connections … into links between beginnings and endings. And between each other of course. Connecting each beginning to … well, potentially to all the endings … so you'd have to program in some selectable parameters, limits. And you'd have to be able to select for length: number of words, or number of scenes, or something. Not a fixed number — a range. But those are just details.*

The middle would be the largest section, by far — just imagine how many ways there could be to get from any plot beginning to any ending! Maybe that's the only section that would need layers. Or … maybe you'd just need a beginning and an end — maybe the program could imagine the middle.

So ... you pick a beginning. Or an end. Or both. Select any options you want. Then you click "START." The scenes sort themselves into sequenced patterns. And they appear on screens. Each pattern is a different plot, a different story. Then ... you just open one you like, and it will present a video outline of the plot, seamless. Maybe with text: descriptions or dialogue. You could just fine-tune that output, or instruct the program to write your story from it. Or you could use that as an outline to write your story. Or novel, or screenplay. Or poem, even. If it's not going well, just open another one. Of course you could save any one you've put aside.

He searches our eyes, seeking comprehension.

He's imagining, creating. He's not writing the code — code is just a way to get from A to B. Code is just the circulation; he's creating the heart, the organs, the body — the whole organism.

A million scenes and plots expand exponentially, filling the room.

It could be done; it would need only the algorithm. And many, many inputs, of course. But it could be done.

(Loosely based on a conversation with M. Chaudhury in 2010. Since then, several sophisticated plot-development programs have been designed and are in use)

Last of the Ploughmen

*Y*ou *there! Get out of his way!"* Dad's parade-sergeant voice boomed down from the upper-level deck.
Startled, I stumbled and fell backwards. I cradled Mum's Kodak Brownie in my arms — better to break a leg than the treasured camera she used to record her family's history! Raising an enormous hoof for his next step, the plough-horse glared at me and snorted. I quickly rolled down the slope out of his path.

Calgary, 1946. I was eight-and-a-half. Dad had come home from overseas in November of '45, so this was his first spring back.

Somehow Mum had held things together for most of five years, struggling to raise four kids under ten — dealing with teachers and homework and medical emergencies, knitting and sewing, washing and cooking. She had traded ration coupons with neighbours, cadged soup bones ("for the dog") from the understanding butcher, and occasionally bought groceries on the tab till the next Army cheque arrived.

With sometimes-grudging help from the oldest two, George and me, she had always managed to grow some vegetables and a few flowers at the sides of the house. But the main part of the property, the half-acre or so that slanted from the back of the house down to the lane, lay fallow, beyond her ability to tame. She'd rented out a small plot to a couple in a trailer, who shared our bathroom (she had to provide them with toilet paper — otherwise they used newspapers and blocked the pipes); beyond that it was unproductive. With the man of the house back home, it was time to reclaim it and grow a proper garden again. Hence the ploughing.

"What are you playing at?" Dad shouted down.

"Nothing," I called back. I had been trying to take pictures of the man and beast that were transforming the overgrown prairie sod back into Dad's garden. That was what Mum did: took pictures of the people and events of our lives.

Besides extended family and friends and neighbours, she had shots of her flowers, the tracks being torn up when the South Calgary streetcars were replaced by buses, and our scruffy mutt Butch. But there was no use trying to explain that to him.

I didn't know much about my father — mostly he was just a big gruff presence with strict ways and little patience. I kept out of his way as much as I could. Was he like that before the war? — I didn't remember.

I whistled to big brother, ten-year-old George, who was up by the house. He called up to the deck, getting permission to go and play. Then he and little sister Phyllis and littler brother Howard came running down the edge of the yard inside the wire fence. We watched the ploughing from the cover of the spreading caragana canopy that served as our cabin, castle, or forest (as required). Last year's long thin seed pods that we called bananas had dried up and curled open. This year's small yellow flowers were barely in bud.

The ploughman and his plodding animal cut a deep, neat furrow across one way, then turned and cut a lower furrow across the other way. Every time they swung around in front of us, it looked as if the horse's monstrous hair-draped hooves were going to trample us in our hiding place! I'd never seen ploughing close-up before — I was so fascinated I forgot to take pictures. The man blended in with the neutral earth: faded check shirt, baggy grey pants, muddy boots, and beat-up brown straw hat shading his leathery face. The pungent odours of horse droppings and sweat hung in the air.

When they'd worked their way to the bottom of the yard, the man wrestled the plough onto its side and got the horse to drag it back up to the top. Dad brought the animal a bucket of water. Mum brought the man a dipper and a cup of tea. There were nods of thanks, but few if any words. The men had a quiet smoke. We knew Dad came from a homesteading family; maybe this farmer did too, and they understood each other without speaking.

Or maybe it was just that plain men didn't have a lot to say in those days. Dad didn't talk much about the war, anyway. Sometimes we heard of places he'd been overseas. Most of the stories were about the old-fashioned towns, the landscape, and the hospitality of the people. Some were anecdotes from camps and billets. We never heard about the fighting.

The man unfastened the plough from the harness and hitched up a spike harrow. He stood on the rugged steel frame to add weight, and the routine started over: across one way, turn downhill, across the other way. Phyllis giggled, "It's a side-hill dodger!" That was a well-known part of Alberta mythology: a furry animal with shorter legs on one side than on the other, so it could go around steep foothills without falling over. Of course each one could go around in only one direction. (In one version, the boy dodgers could go only one way and the girl dodgers the other way. Any implications that might have had for reproduction were totally lost on us.)

George replied with grown-up disdain, "It's not, silly, it's a horse. Can't you see its legs are all the same?"

"But it's on a hill! Why doesn't it tip over then?" But six-year-olds don't always get their questions answered, even logical ones.

Ploughing and harrowing — trudging from one side of the property to the other and back again, over and over — eventually grew boring to watch. Shielded by the caragana, we crawled under the fence and escaped into the double vacant lot next door. Beyond the vacant lot lived Brian Smith's family with their purebred spaniels.

The wide expanse of wintered grass between us and the Smiths was brown and matted. I bent down and grabbed a handful — I thought it felt dry enough for the burn-off. Burning off the previous year's dried grass to prevent prairie fires dated back to the early settlers, we'd been told. I remembered watching the men and older boys the year before. They dragged a burning branch through the grass, then allowed only the upwind line of flame to burn, checked by the headwind and skillfully-wielded wet burlap sacks. Grey-white wisps of sweet grass smoke drifted across the landscape. I couldn't wait till I was old enough to help.

With big brother in the lead, we four adventurers explored our territory. Howard had the shortest legs (and the most interest in tiny things), so George was always after him to keep up. We investigated around the vacant field and down to the back lane, then meandered the length of the lane across the bottom of our yard.

Along the way there were all kinds of wonders to take in: pigweed, thistles, dandelions, and buffalo beans; robins and meadowlarks; and lots of insects and spiders. (The grasshoppers were waiting for the heat of summer.) We also spotted a watchful gopher, a slithering garter snake, a mangy dog, and a couple of stray cats. We saw old Mrs. Grenville spading her Victory Garden. George and I admired Mr. Switzer's black Dodge car that he'd brought out of storage with the end of gasoline rationing.

Finally, we headed home through the rickety gate at the bottom corner of our property. When we got there, the ploughman and his horse and equipment were gone. The freshly-cultivated garden smelled moist and earthy.

Dad was sitting in his armchair, reading. "Is the grass next door ready for the burn-off?" I asked him.

He didn't look up from his paper. "We'll see. Have to get the spuds in first." I knew about potatoes from the few hills Mum had grown every year, seeded from the last of the previous year's crop.

The rest of the spring, and the whole summer and fall, seemed to be filled with onerous labour. There were different jobs for different-sized workers: digging, hoeing, raking, planting, weeding, watering, picking off caterpillars and potato bugs by hand; then more watering and weeding. But the work paid off. Through the late summer and fall we harvested fresh vegetables and berries; then all winter we had a cold-cellar full of potatoes and root crops, and homemade preserves from Mum's pressure cooker.

The garden wasn't the only thing developing with the man of the house back home. In August we got a new baby sister, Grace.

* * *

The next spring a brash young man in a black cowboy hat came to plough. He didn't have a horse — he had a dirty red Massey-Harris tractor that made a big racket and spewed stinky black smoke from its upright stack.

His furrows weren't nearly as straight as the older man's. Even I could see that.

Like It Was on Tracks

L et me tell you a curling story. Happened last Saturday. It's the last end. We're tied at five each, and they've got two rocks counting. But we have the last rock, the hammer.

Our skip and vice have spent half an hour, it seems like, discussing strategy. But there's not really much to discuss. There are a lot of rocks in play. The way everything is lined up, there's no decent possibility of a take-out, and we don't have anything we can raise. It looks like the only shot is a nearly impossible in-turn finesse: slide through the outer port, with maybe half an inch to spare; get past the rest of the junk, and draw to the button in between their two shot rocks. Plan B? — there isn't one.

The skip slides up the side of the sheet with his usual worried frown. He settles in the hack and studies the house. He tips his rock and cleans the bottom with his brush. Twice: once to clean it, once just out of habit. He signals the vice to give him an inch more ice. The vice shifts his brush almost imperceptibly. The skip re-aligns his shoulders to the brush, then studies some more: focusing, concentrating. Finally, he draws the rock back and pushes off.

He's good out of the hack: nice extension, smooth delivery, perfect line. But at the last instant he second-guesses himself and pulls his release a bit. Before the rock even clears the first hog line, we're all thinking it hasn't got quite enough weight. "It's light!" he yells — "Sweep it!"

The lead and I are already on it. I'm almost tucked in under the front of the rock, where I like to sweep. His brush is two inches ahead of mine. We work well together.

"Hurry hard!" the vice is shouting at us. "Hurry, hurry hard!" I feel like telling him, *I've done this before, y'know — you want this brush up your ice?* But I save my breath. I just keep sweeping, bearing down hard on my brush. Slicking the sheet in front of the rock, willing it to go as far as it possibly can.

"Sweep it, sweep it! All the way!" the skip yells. I'm probably too old to be working this hard, but I'm sweeping on adrenaline now. The arena is filled with their shouts: *"Hurry hard! Sweep it! All the way, don't stop! Sweep it!"*

It's over the hog line. Somehow it gets through all the guards, with about a hair's clearance from a couple of them. There isn't enough room for two brushes in the house, so the lead lifts his out. I keep at it as long as I can. Finally, the rock curls to a stop — right between their two, actually touching one of them. Dead on the button. A win by one.

It was a beautiful shot, a perfect shot. The skip and vice are elated. "Great sweeping, guys!" they both call out, beaming. Which it was, and it's good to hear. But the best thing was just seeing that rock respond: seeing it keep moving when it couldn't possibly go any farther; and at the end, seeing it gently curl right into place. Like it was on tracks.

Scientists have tried to measure the effect of sweeping on speed, momentum, curl, everything. Some of them say it doesn't really influence the shot. But every curler knows better.

The Boulevard

This is the ironic local name for the mile-long stretch of gravel roadway that connects the paved streets of the town proper with the dirt track that leads eastward to a few hard-scrabble farms (and, eventually, to the next township). The concrete sidewalks are broken and uneven, the cracks nurturing a spindly crop of opportunistic weeds. A strip of run-down businesses, low-rent housing and empty shells, it is neither suburban nor rural – it's the kind of neglected in-between place that develops a perverse character of its own. By daylight it is merely unsightly; but when night falls it becomes an eerie setting of nervous emptiness and shadowy threats.

* * *

In the daytime, we things serve the incomprehensible needs of the fleshies. But at night The Boulevard is our territory. My territory, to be more accurate: my domain. I am Gravel.

Quiet night, I sent out to nothing in particular.

Damn slow night, I could use some action. Pole 1536 with his same old complaint. He's old and wooden, lives in the past. And he's stuck there in one spot, doesn't have the length and flow that I have. Sure, his sagging wires connect him to his kind, but it's not the same.

Couldn't we all, it's not just you! I resisted pointing out his obvious limitations. One of my kinder times: I'm well-known for my sharpness.

Curbing woke up, a bit late on the uptake as usual. *You two having a pissing contest?* She had little idea what the expression meant: it was just something she'd picked up from the fleshies' constant chatter.

Guy talk, Pole chided. *Go back to sleep.*

I won't. You're not the boss of me.

I flashed a glint at Pole to keep him from retorting, and glared at her. *Behave yourself*, I warned her with a nudge of my sharp edges. *This is still my Boulevard.*

Yes, Sir.

Funny thing, that is. Curbing doesn't realize that in fact she prevents my expanding on either side. I trained her fast, when I first came in and she was hardly dried. Showed her who was in charge. Any time she gets uppity, I just get her confused between her north and south sides – keeps her unsure of herself for several nights.

It wasn't easy taking charge of the place at first. When we were all new there was a lot of competition for control: we pushed and jostled and sent rude, boastful messages from dusk to dawn. But I played it smart. Got Curbing unsure that way, the Poles another way, the Sidewalks another way; played one against the other. I even convinced them I was here from the beginning, sent by Quarry, the deity. When nothing really knows or remembers, you can establish any belief system you want, as long as you're consistent and bold enough to sell it. My central position helped a lot, but it's all in how you use your strengths. It didn't even matter when I started to get packed down and some of my bits got smaller and rounded. I just acted as confident and authoritative as ever, and nothing even noticed.

Will everything PLEASE shut up and go to sleep? Hydrant E43, whining as usual. *I dunno about you guys, but I have to be alert in the morning!*

Yeah, yeah, I sent back. *Like every other muckin' morning, when you stand around preening and doing nothing! Just cool your water, we're having a conversation here.* He sighed.

Suddenly Grass-strip yelped, *Ouch!* One of those strange "plate" things had come flying out from an upper hole of the nearest Building and landed on one of her sections. She was so brown and dry I'd almost forgotten she could still feel anything.

Pole sent, *Great, some action!*

It's not funny, Grass-strip whimpered. *That really hurt!*

Pole was practically chortling. *Woke you up, did it? You dried-up old hag!*

You are SO mean! And stupid – YOU'RE the one who's dried-up!

Pole drew himself up to his considerable height. *I am*

NOT. I am properly aged. You, my dear, are past your best-by date. Way past it.

You're a … a dried-up old stick-in the-mud!

I have maturity and character. And depth – you are a shallow-rooted bitch!

You're a smelly old dog-pee toilet!

You are a fetid desiccated dung-heap!

In Quarry's name, just SHUT UP, both of you! I sent with my full authority. Witless bickering is so tiresome.

I decided to check out the area farther east, towards Dirt Track. (Not that I'd ever associate with him.) I signalled Curbing to flow her awareness with me. But I was interrupted by more "dishes" flying from the opening, gliding down almost gracefully. They landed on Grass-strip and Sidewalk and even on me. *Grit!* I cursed. *Stone-damned fleshies!*

Of course that made Grass-strip feel vindicated. *See, I told you it hurt!*

Sod off, Grass-strip, I never even felt it. I'm heading east. They hated that – Curbing and the Sidewalks and I seem to be able to keep our physical places but flow our awareness east or west, in a way the others can't.

But it was not to be. Suddenly Pole broadcast with great urgency, *Fire! Fire!* Sure enough, our terrible nemesis had landed inside the same opening the dishes had come from.

Without thinking, I firmed myself to carry an anti-Fire machine. Curbing trembled and Grass-strip began to whimper. None of us had a lot of experience with Fire, though we had seen a few minor incidents over the years. As usual, I took charge. *Curbing – hold the line, both sides! Grass-strip – heavy boots coming, be brave! Sidewalks – boots and big machines, firm up! Hydrant – stand by for hoses!* I barely remembered the last time this had happened – I simply issued the most practical commands I could think of, as if I'd been laid down just for such an emergency. I was in my glory.

Panicky fleshie squeals came from the orange-streaked hole, followed by the creatures themselves streaming out the bottom opening. They scuttled across to the opposite Sidewalk, where they milled around in disarray like grotesquely huge ants without a queen.

When the anti-Fire machine arrived, flashing its lights and screaming, it put way more weight on me than any of the usual fleshie machines, even the farm tractors; and it had no hesitation about braking hard and bruising me. But I held firm, doing my duty. The armoured fleshies hooked up to Hydrant E43 and started pouring water into the upper hole in the Building.

Fire was soon contained, and eventually was knocked out. The quick response of the anti-Fire fleshies had prevented him from spreading to more of the Building. His lust for complete destruction thwarted, he disappeared skyward in trails of angry sparks and clouds of dirty soot. The anti-Fire fleshies climbed out of their protective shells and did some kind of ceremony that involved smacking each others' limbs, then rolled up their hoses and packed everything back onto the machine. As they clambered aboard, the one who appeared to be in charge slipped and fell off, cutting its hands badly on some of my flinty pieces. While I was used to the usual drips of oil and such, I found its red fleshie-juice slimy and disgusting. Its noises told me it was angry, but it didn't need to take it out on me with kicking. It yelled something that sounded as if it wanted the whole world paved over.

The anti-Fire machine took off, with quite unnecessary grinding of its heavy tires. Ignoring the pain, I assessed the damage.

It wasn't too bad. Hydrant was exhausted, naturally, but beaming with pride. Grass-strip was a bit scorched and torn up. The Sidewalks complained, but they were okay, nothing worse than some heavy scuffing. Curbing had been kicked in the sides and was feeling very sorry for herself – she'd need extra attention for the next little while. The Building was smoke-streaked and wet; but it wasn't in our inner circle anyway. The worst casualty among us was Pole 1536: a few embers had lodged in some of his age-cracks and burned quite deeply before they'd gone out. He was weakened and sore, but he'd survive.

It was very late by then. The faint lightening of the eastern sky foretold the end of night. I broadcast a good-morning message, praising everything for their courage under extreme duress and wishing them a peaceful rest, in the name of Quarry. I cued Curbing to send the traditional lullaby that I'd composed many years earlier.

* * *

Smarting from his embarrassment over falling off the truck, the Fire Captain took his concerns about the condition of The Boulevard to the Fire Chief, who was his brother-in-law. The Chief had a long talk with the Reeve, his first cousin and poker buddy, over a couple of cold beers. They agreed that the area was a blight on the township and had been neglected much too long. The Reeve took a proposal for improvements to the fractious Council. As usual, there was neither the budget nor the political will to embark on a proper redevelopment; but they agreed upon a modest upgrade.

So it was that, a few weeks later, a stately procession headed out of town to The Boulevard. Led by the contractor's men in their dirty pick-ups, the parade included a steaming asphalt truck, dump trucks, graders, and a huge float bearing a steamroller and a front-end loader. Around mid-afternoon the Fire Captain drove out in the Department's big red Dodge Ram to observe it for himself: the paving-over of that damned mile-long strip of gravel that had cut his hands. He was gloating.

The other things missed Gravel, missed his wisdom and firm authority. But eventually they adjusted. As things do.

About the Author

John Ambury, a prize-winning poet in high school, returned to creative writing in 2009 after a hiatus of more than 50 years. His output is eclectic: by turns experiential and existential, descriptive and interpretive, philosophical and whimsical. While always thoughtful, it is accessible rather than obscure. In form it ranges from Elizabethan sonnets through rhyming couplets, linked rhyme and haiku to free verse (currently his form of choice). He is experimenting with short story writing. His poems have been published in numerous anthologies and periodicals; this is his first solo collection.

John is associated with The Ontario Poetry Society (Executive), the Writers and Editors Network (former Board member), the League of Canadian Poets (Associate), the Canadian Federation of Poets, the Courtneypark Literary Circle, the Oakville Literary Alliance (Lit Café), and 100,000 Poets for Change (former Committee member). He is a frequent reader at Ontario poetry events, from London to Oakville to Oshawa. He freelances as a proofreader, editor and book reviewer, and has been a poetry contest judge.

A retired printing ink technician, technical writer, and chemical sales representative, John holds a Professional Grade in the Oil & Colour Chemists' Association. He is currently (as well as a writer) a small-business owner, a travelling technical speaker, a part-time professional actor, and an enthusiastic amateur curler.

John is a native of Alberta, a former Kingstonian, and a long-time resident of Toronto.

CPSIA information can be obtained
at www.ICGtesting.com
Printed in the USA
LVOW01s0149200516

489127LV00014B/112/P

9 781926 926636